IMAGES
of America

REMEMBERING THE
CALDWELLS

Grover Cleveland

Grover Cleveland, born in Caldwell, New Jersey, March 18, 1837, was the 22nd and 24th President of the United States.

This drawing of Grover Cleveland and his birthplace was done by noted local artist Rachel A. Farrington. The birthplace, now a state and national historic site, is located on Bloomfield Avenue near Arlington Avenue, Caldwell. A replica of the drawing was made into a medallion to be used for the 150th anniversary of the birth of Grover Cleveland.

IMAGES
of America

REMEMBERING THE
CALDWELLS

John J. Collins

ARCADIA
PUBLISHING

Published by Arcadia Publishing
Charleston, South Carolina

Library of Congress Catalog Card Number: 2006923520

For all general information contact Arcadia Publishing at:
Telephone 843-853-2070
Fax 843-853-0044
E-mail sales@arcadiapublishing.com
For customer service and orders:
Toll-Free 1-888-313-2665

Visit us on the Internet at www.arcadiapublishing.com

*The net proceeds of this book will benefit
the Grover Cleveland Birthplace Memorial Association.*

CONTENTS

ACKNOWLEDGMENTS

My deepest appreciation is extended to two good friends whose support and assistance have made this book a reality: Alyce Burdette Batta, for her considerable time and dedication, as well as her computer expertise and invaluable contribution in transcribing the text; and E. Leslie Byrnes, former resident and town historian, who so generously entrusted me with his valuable collection of postcards and vintage images and graciously shared his vast knowledge of the area.

A special thanks to longtime resident and historian Dorothy Budd Bartle for her encouragement and input. In addition, I wish to thank Ruth Crane Shepard, Robert Williams, Beverly W. Crifasi, Ph.D., W. David Gibson, Ph.D., Richard Gibbs, and the friendly folks at Caldwell Photo. Appreciation is also given to Roxanne Douglas and the West Caldwell Historical Society, Yvonne Goodhill and the North Caldwell Historical Society, Sister Rita Margaret, Naomi Eisenberger, Robert Norris, Franco DiGangi, Clare Pennington, the libraries of Caldwell and West Caldwell, and posthumously to the late Grace Gore and Jack Hull. I am grateful to all who shared their memories and to Arcadia Publishing for allowing me to present these images to our friends, old and new.

INTRODUCTION

The Caldwells were settled in the early 18th century by pioneers who moved westward from Newark or through the Passaic Valley from the "Dutch" areas of Bergen County. While it was thought that the way had been cleared by Newark's 1702 purchase of this Horse Neck Tract from the Lenape Indians, clear land titles were clouded by the counter claims of the Proprietors. The resulting Horse Neck Riots of the 1740s were among the earliest American challenges to Royal authority.

Local hamlets clustered around churches and schools in this outlying section of Newark, and it was not until 1798 that the bulk of the Horse Neck Tract was designated Caldwell Township.

The 19th century saw dramatic changes taking place in our area, many the consequence of the construction of the "Big Road," Bloomfield Avenue. Israel Crane's stock company pushed the toll road through to Caldwell by 1808 and it became the main link with the markets in Newark for all that lay to the west.

As early as the 1850s some city folks were finding that these beautiful western slopes of the Second Mountain, with abundant pure water and equally clear air, were a delightful place to spend their summer months. In time, Caldwell would be promoted as the "Denver of the East," and to accommodate the influx of seasonal visitors, hotels and boarding houses multiplied and became a dominant aspect of both the economy and the ambience, alike. The Monomonock Inn, opened in 1901, ultimately came to be the most conspicuous representative of this phenomenon.

Further bolstering the economy was Caldwell's position as a major farming area with the expected supporting mills and stores. Then, with the arrival of the railroad in 1891, the area was firmly linked to the population centers to the east.

7

And not to be overlooked was Caldwell's most conspicuous contribution to the Nation—the 22nd and 24th President of the United States, Grover Cleveland.

The Caldwells have grown, the dirt roads have been paved, the railroad abandoned, and most of the lodging homes are gone, but the beauty of the Caldwells remains. Various communities recognize their past through their remaining historic landmarks. Although the Caldwells have lost a number of their early and most fascinating sites, some survive and stand their ground firmly as silent testimonials to an almost forgotten era. Many of the people of the Caldwells made significant contributions in molding our communities and some paid the ultimate price while defending the liberties and freedom of our nation.

The following pages are not meant to be a history but rather a look back in time to the proud and resourceful heritage of the Caldwells through the use of historic images. Enjoy your journey through Old Caldwell.

BIBLIOGRAPHY

Curry, Sister Lois. *Women after His Own Heart*. Brooklyn, N.Y.: New City Press, 1981.

Brydon, Norman F. *Reverend James Caldwell, Patriot 1734–1781*. Caldwell, N.J.: Caldwell Bicentennial Committee, 1976.

Claire, Sister Loretta and Brydon, Norman F. *CALDWELL . . . Yesterday . . . Today, 1776–1976*. Morristown, N.J.: Mark Lithographers, 1976.

Lockward, Lynn G. *A Puritan Heritage, The First Presbyterian Church in Horse Neck*. Caldwell, N.J.: N.p., 1955.

New Jersey Writer's Project. *Caldwell History from Pioneer Days*. Caldwell, N.J.: Progress Publishing Company, 1938.

Norwood, Benjamin Robert. *Old Caldwell—A Retrospect, 1699–1926*. Caldwell, N.J.: Progress Publishing Co., 1927.

Shaw, William H.. *History of Essex and Hudson Counties, New Jersey*, Vol. I. Philadelphia: Everts and Peck, 1884.

One

THE PEOPLE

During the 1928 presidential campaign, Mr. and Mrs. Herbert Hoover made a brief stop at the Grover Cleveland birthplace. The group includes soon-to-be Governor Morgan Larsen; Hamilton Kean, who later became a senator; Senator Walter Edge; and Verona Mayor David Slayback. After a short ceremony and signing of the register, enthusiastic crowds watched as the Hoovers took an auto tour of the area.

Birthplace of Ex-President Cleveland, Caldwell, N. J.

After four years of negotiations, the parsonage of the Caldwell Presbyterian Church and birthplace of President Grover Cleveland was sold to the Grover Cleveland Birthplace Memorial Association on March 18, 1913.

Richard F. Cleveland, son of Grover Cleveland, received a large brass ceremonial key to open the door and take possession on behalf of the association. Esther Cleveland, his sister, entered at the same time with a floral wreath.

Celebration was evident in Caldwell. A parade through town and an elaborately decorated manse was in honor of the birthplace being sold to the Grover Cleveland Birthplace Memorial Association.

The association had difficulty in securing funds to maintain the birthplace property. Consequently, they gave the property to the state of New Jersey on October 6, 1934. The building was completely renovated and restored to its condition c. 1870. The work was done in 1936, during the Depression, by E. Leslie Byrnes Sr. under the WPA at a cost of about $10,000.

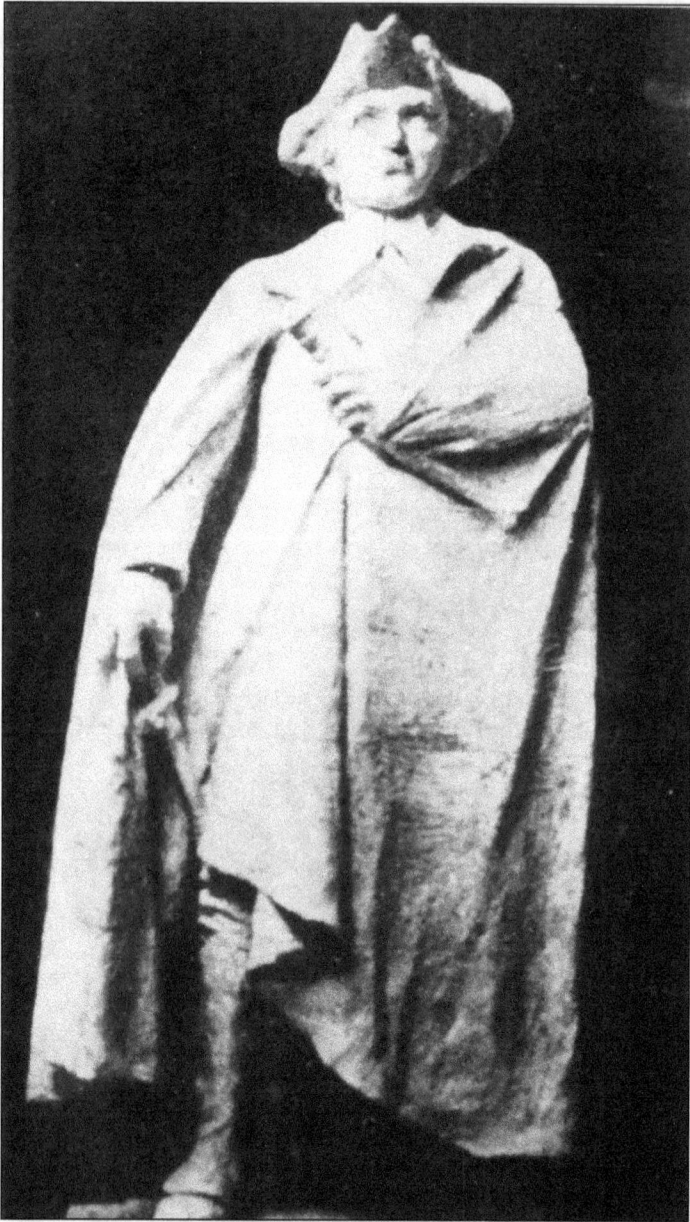

The Reverend James Caldwell, for whom the town of Caldwell was named, was born on April 17, 1734, in Cub Creek, Virginia. After graduating from Princeton in 1759, he married Hannah Ogden, whom he had first met when he was a student at the College of New Jersey. Together they raised nine children. He frequently presided at the old Presbyterian church at Caldwell and also served as a chaplain in the Revolution War. Hannah was killed by a British soldier in June of 1780. Legend has it that, during the Battle of Springfield, he saw his army's men slacking for want of gun wadding. He galloped to the church at Springfield and brought the hymn books to the soldiers and shouted, "Now put Watts into them, boys!" This event is also reported as "Give 'Em Watts, boys," referring to Issac Watts, a prolific composer of hymns who died in 1748. The result was that the American soldiers were victorious. The Reverend James Caldwell was killed in Elizabeth in November 1781 by a shot from a sentinel.

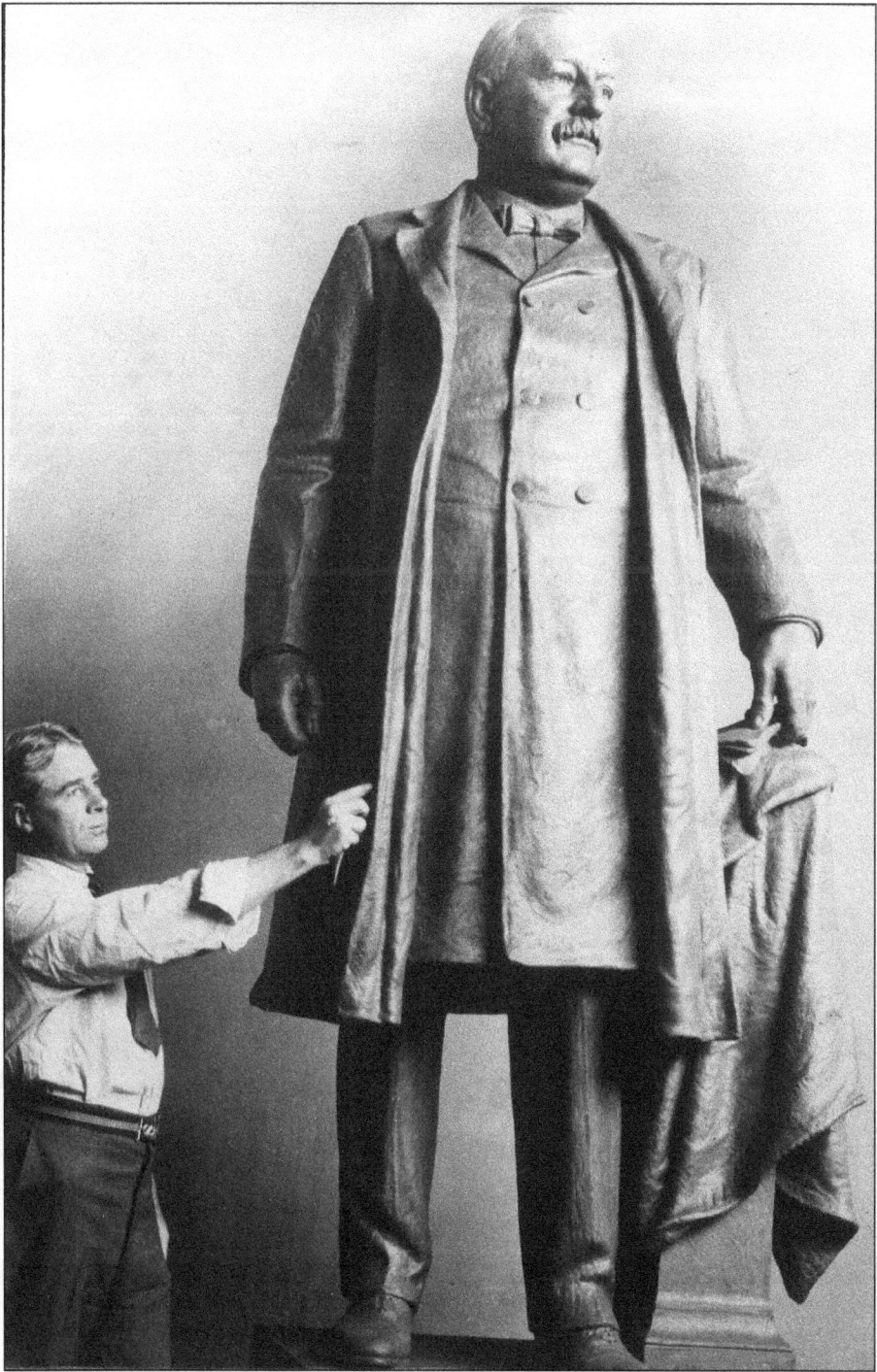

This bronze statue of President Grover Cleveland was unveiled during the Buffalo Centennial Exposition in 1932. The sculptor, Bryant Baker of New York, posed here with his work. (Photo courtesy of John A. Sullivan III.)

When Lewis G. Lockward took the oath of office as the first mayor of Caldwell Borough in 1892, there were fewer than a dozen stores, all of which were of frame construction. There were no sidewalks and no street lights; only one telephone in the drug store served the needs of the entire village. Much has changed since that inauguration.

Charlotte Williams Personette was the daughter of Abram Personette (caretaker of the old burial grounds behind the Presbyterian church, and, in 1881, the last person to be buried there). She married prominent physician Dr. John T. Lockward, and their son, Lewis G. Lockward, became the Caldwell's first mayor. Upon the death of Dr. Lockward, Charlotte married Calvin G. Backus. She was also the great-grandmother of Dorothy Budd Bartle of Caldwell, the present head of the Grover Cleveland Birthplace Memorial Association.

A one-horse power mower! In this c. 1908 photo, Michael Zelek Sr. is pictured cutting one of the extensive lawns of the Leaycraft House, an estate that burned down in the late 1920s.

Jonathan Sylvester Provost, a member of one of Caldwell's most prominent families of the time, cuts a dashing figure in this horseless buggy, c. 1906.

Caldwell automobile mechanic and salesman Frank Leonard tries out one of his "new" cars, *c.* 1910. Leonard is pictured in front of his Roseland Avenue garage. He later moved to Bloomfield Avenue.

This 1935 photograph shows a group of Scouts in front of the old Caldwell Municipal Building on Roseland Avenue with borough clerk Lasalle Jacobus (left) and Mayor Joseph Dosch (right). The event was Boys Week, when the Scouts would fill town positions for a day.

Dr. Edward E. Peck was mayor of the borough of Caldwell during World War I and died while in office. The memorial on the Caldwell Commons defines the man as follows: "Edward Everitt Peck, M.D., 1859–1918, Faithful Physician, Loyal Citizen, Efficient Public Servant. Friend of Man. Testimonial of the esteem and affection from the people of West Essex."

The history of the Caldwell Pharmacy is much akin to the history of the borough. This building was a former schoolhouse that was renovated into a drug store. The pharmacy was established in 1875 by Lester A. Wyatt. In 1881, it was bought by Dr. Edward E. Peck. The pharmacy's name was changed to Hasler's Pharmacy when it was purchased by William N. Hasler in 1881, to be followed by his brother, Herman Hasler. The author operated the pharmacy from 1955 to 1994, when the Hasler Pharmacy era ended in the Caldwells.

EDWARD EVERETT PECK. M. D.
1859 ✚ 1918

FAITHFUL PHYSICIAN - LOYAL CITIZEN
- EFFICIENT PUBLIC SERVANT -
- FRIEND OF MAN -

A TESTIMONIAL OF ESTEEM AND AFFECTION
FROM THE PEOPLE OF WESTERN ESSEX

The memorial for Dr. Peck stands on the Caldwell Commons.

Sporting activities, baseball in particular, were an integral part of the the lives of the people of the Caldwells. The first recorded baseball team, the Rurals, was organized in the 1870s with every team member being a Caldwell man. This vintage photo of the 1909 Caldwell Athletic League Baseball Team includes the following, from left to right: (kneeling) E. Brewer, H. Hipfelt, H. Clawson, W. Wasmer, and J. Phaler; (standing) Jim Adams, F. Hartman, A. Webber, J. Gosman, G. Schwartz, and Paul Albright.

These young women comprised the Kardettes basketball team in 1932. The Kardettes played other women's teams in the area at the Grover Cleveland High School. Team members appear from left to right as follows: (front row) Cecelia Bechinsky Washington, Bobby Ashton, and Luella Van Dyk Greason; (back row) Stacia Bechinsky DeOld, Florence White Lyon, Eva Betcher, and Florence Mowrey Cubby.

20

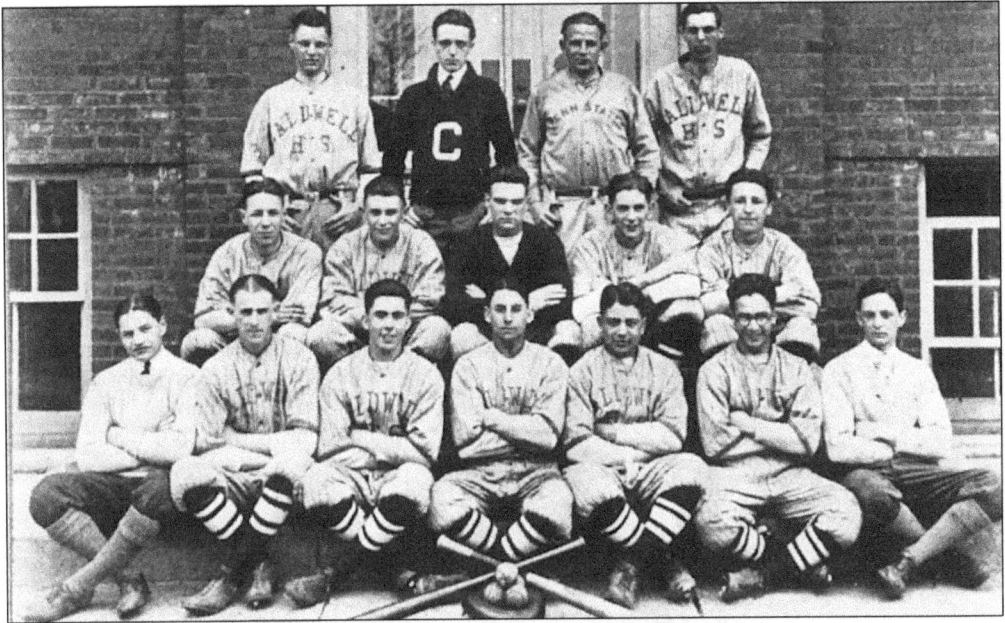

In the spring of 1923, Caldwell High School's baseball team, under the direction of Coach Charles Brumbaugh, fielded a team with Jim Cozier as captain. The team included Brad Behrman, catcher; Bill Hicken and Frank DePaolo, pitchers; LaSalle Jacobus, first base; Fairbanks MacCormack, second base; Fred Mitchell, third base; and Joseph Schiavone, short stop. In the field were James Cozier, Milton Cooper, Gordon Graham, and Raymond Miller. The managers were Stetter, Galusha, and Harris.

In 1923, Coach Charles Brumbaugh was at a disadvantage; since he had no gymnasium, basketball practices were held at Kingsley School, Essex Fells, and all games were played away from home. Only one game was won, that being against Irvington High School, although there were several closely contested games.

Zenas C. Crane was born on October 22, 1804, at the homestead in Caldwell and spent his entire life in the immediate neighborhood. He was a Victorian entrepreneur involved in farming, the tobacco industry, tanning, shoe manufacturing, the Crane sawmill, and the management of the Caldwell Hotel. He married Mary Harrison in 1833 and their children were Marcus H., Caleb, and Anna Maria. His son Caleb managed the farm during the Civil War.

The homestead of Zenas C. Crane was completed in 1854 and replaced the original family home that burned in 1848. The structure, which still stands on the west end of Westville Avenue, is occupied by the West Caldwell Historical Society and is owned by the town of West Caldwell.

A citizen's committee of the Franklin and Westville districts was formed in 1892 to take the preliminary steps towards forming a new borough. Not until 1904 were the boundaries established and accepted. The newly incorporated borough was named West Caldwell. Caleb Crane, son of Zenas C. Crane, was elected West Caldwell's first mayor and held that office until 1909.

Reverend Richard Falley Cleveland, the fifth child of William Cleveland and Margaret Falley, was born in Connecticut in June 1805. After graduating from Yale, he studied Theology and was ordained in 1828. While stationed in Portsmith, Virginia, Mr. Cleveland decided to accept the call of the Caldwell Presbyterian Church and was installed as pastor in the latter part of May 1834. On March 18, 1837, in the back room of the parsonage, a son was born whose future career would have national importance. The boy was named Stephen Grover Cleveland in honor of the first pastor of the church. Later in life, he omitted Stephen from his name.

The Bartlett Post of the Grand Army of the Republic was formed by Civil War veterans in 1878. In the 1880s, the post built "GAR Hall" to serve as a meeting place. Although it was little more than a barn, it served as the only meeting place in the village for 20 years.

John Harrison, a collector for the Prudential Insurance Company, is pictured standing at the trolley loop on the corner of Bloomfield and Central Avenues. His private rig is on his left. Note the attractive waiting room building in the background.

In 1900, during the administration of Mayor John Espy, the Caldwell Volunteer Fire Department was organized with Cornelius Hoage as chief. As time went on, many merchants made monthly voluntary contributions to support the department. In 1916, the department was headed by Chief Moran, and after several requests, an up-to-date firetruck was purchased.

In 1911, a new firetruck was purchased, the modern horse-drawn fire apparatus of the time. "Alice and Edna," a team of grey mares owned by Frederick Cook, were hitched to the hook and ladder before going off to a fire.

This horse-drawn fire fighting equipment was purchased by the Town of West Caldwell in 1913. Shown with this team of white horses are Arthur Herzog (holding the reins), Elmer Harrison (holding the son of Alson VanNess), and Theodore Kanouse. Mr. VanNess is pictured here standing beside the vehicle.

The Borough of West Caldwell purchased its first motorized fire apparatus in 1917 for $4,200. The old firehouse on Bloomfield Avenue had to be remodeled to accommodate it. From left to right are Roswell Conklin, J.E. Baldwin (the driver), I.H. VanNess, Earl VanNess, Horace Welchman, and Arthur Herzog proudly showing off their new "rig."

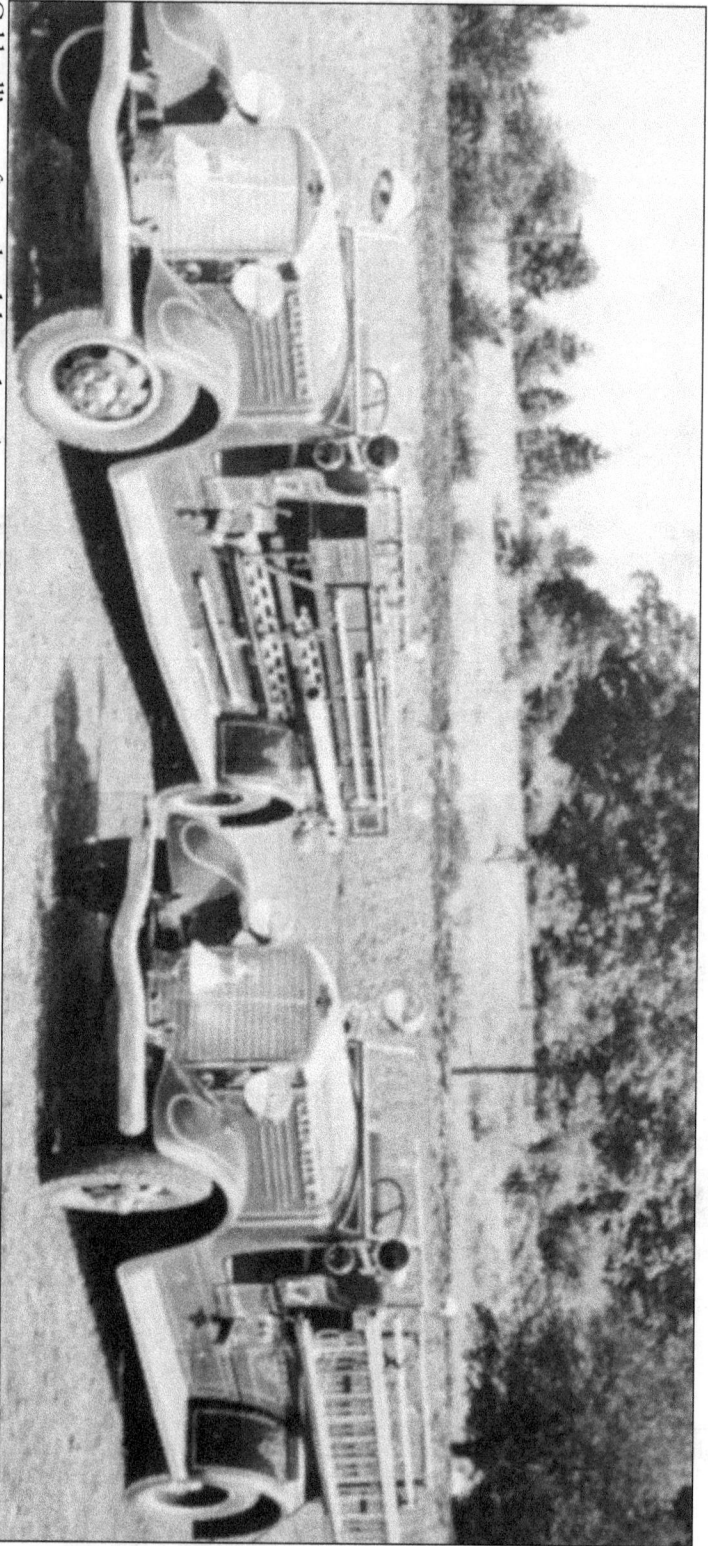

Caldwell's new firetrucks, delivered on August 1, 1937, were parked on the Kiwanis Oval to have their picture taken. These two American-LaFrance firetrucks were the first new trucks since a Seagrave was purchased in 1916. The borough council had appropriated $12,000 for the trucks, but when the cost ran to $13,100, the volunteer fire department made up the difference.

Two

CHURCHES
AND EDUCATION

The Old Meeting House was the first gathering place for the Presbyterian congregation, organized in 1784. The building was completed in 1796, and a steeple was added in 1801. In 1872, the entire structure was destroyed by fire and replaced by a stone building. The image to the right is an artist's rendering of the Old Caldwell Church.

In 1782, a parsonage house was erected with the lower floor used for the minister's residence and the upper for a congregation meeting room. The church was organized in this room in 1784. The congregation was served by itinerant ministers, the most famous being the Reverend James Caldwell, known historically as the Fighting Parson because of his heroic feats in the Revolutionary War in the Battle of Springfield. The first entry in the old parish book was signed by the Reverend James Caldwell in 1779. In 1788, Reverend Steven Grover was ordained and came to serve as the first regular minister. The parsonage house served until 1796, when a new meetinghouse was built on the present site of the church. After the structure was destroyed by a fire in 1872, the church was rebuilt in brown stone from the Yost Quarry, Eagle Rock Avenue in Pleasantdale, under the leadership of Reverend Charles Berry, pastor. It was completed in 1874. (Photo courtesy of Jim Lent.)

The first building, *c.* 1852, became home to the growing population of the Baptist Church. The first house, pictured to the right, was used as the parsonage.

The original structure was moved to the back of the church property and faced Forest Avenue.

The first Catholic church in Caldwell, St. Aloysius was dedicated November 24, 1892, and located across the street from the present brick church on Bloomfield Avenue. The first Catholic school was established at the same site. Father James Nolan was the first pastor after serving as chaplin to the Sisters of St. Dominic, who have been teaching students at St. Aloysius for over one hundred years.

Construction on the present St. Aloysius Church began in 1922 and was completed toward the end of 1923. The impressive brick structure replaced the small wooden church originally located on the other side of Bloomfield Avenue. Participants in the ceremony were William O'Dowd (with the spade) and the three men behind him, James E. Minschull, Thomas J. Moran, and Harry Smith. The priest to the left is the Reverend Thomas J. McEnery, pastor.

The First Methodist Church was incorporated in February 1894. Services were originally held in the GAR Hall at the corner of Bloomfield Avenue and present Central Avenue. The Tabernacle on Cleveland Street, the first church building, was dedicated on April 21, 1895. The cornerstone of the church shown here was laid July 1899, and the building was consecrated on March 18, 1900, Grover Cleveland's birthday.

Before 1919, approximately 30 Jewish families living in the Caldwells attended services at the Caldwell Presbyterian Church along with their children, who attended the Sunday school. The Jewish League of Caldwell was eventually organized and the first synagogue was built on Washburn Place. Groundbreaking took place on March 13, 1922, and a one-room stucco building was erected. In 1934, Rabbi Goldman was hired, the first of several rabbis to serve. This was the beginning of the community that now stands proudly as Congregation Agudath Israel of West Essex.

In 1862, a charter was granted for establishing Caldwell Lodge #59. The first meeting place was a room over Mead's General Store on Bloomfield Avenue. With the purchase of the the Grover House Annex in 1914, the lodge moved to Smull Avenue, where it remains today.

This is the close-up view of the medallion seen on the side of the following picture of the marble obelisk. Each soldier received a medallion placed on his grave marker.

This marble obelisk of the Reverend Stephen Grover can be found in the old burial ground next to the Caldwell Presbyterian Church. The total number of interments in the burying ground is 451, the last being Abram Personette, dated May 5, 1881. He was sexton of the church and in charge of the burial ground.

LINCOLN SCHOOL

The Lincoln School, located on Crane Street, is one of the oldest in the Caldwell-West Caldwell school system. This photo, taken in the early 1900s, shows the school before an addition was made. The property was sold by the Presbyterian Church to the board of education, and in 1917, the Lincoln Public School was completed and dedicated. Additions were made in 1947 and 1970.

Roosevelt School. - West Caldwell

Prompted by the large population expansion after World War I, Roosevelt School was built in 1923 and was the first elementary school in West Caldwell. In 1978, the school had to close due to a declining school population at the time. The remaining grade schools are operating at full capacity today. The building now serves as the West Essex Campus of Essex County College.

36

The old one-room schoolhouse on Gould Avenue, North Caldwell, was built around 1870 and served the community for 40 years. It remained in use until 1910, when a two-room school was erected. The abandoned building was then converted for borough use and part of it still exists in the upper portion of the North Caldwell Police Station.

Central School was opened in 1875. There were only four classrooms; the second floor was reserved for the custodian and his family. The school was located at the corner of Prospect Street and Academy Road.

Additions were made to the Central School in 1892 and 1902. It was not until 1904, however, that indoor plumbing was installed.

In 1910, a new high school was erected on Prospect Street between Central School and the cemetery. Central School is visible in the background of this photo.

By 1926, all new additions to the Grover Cleveland High School were complete, and it was open for classes in September. When James Caldwell High School was opened in West Caldwell in 1960, the high school became the Grover Cleveland Middle School.

A photo from the 1911 Caldwell High School yearbook shows the faculty wearing the fashions of the times. The seated ladies are Edith Bougher, Vice Principal Mary Wood, and Martha Elting, the Latin and German teacher. The gentlemen are Principal Clarence "Doc" Hedden and Robert Ryder, the Science and Math teacher.

The Caldwell High School graduating class of 1911 included Eric Dixon, William Crane, Russell Riker, Elsie McNeil, Margretta Key, Edith Pierson, and Ruth Sharwell. Twenty-five percent of the class was college bound. Ms. Sharwell went to Wellesley and Mr. Riker to Stevens College.

The groundbreaking ceremony for the motherhouse and novitiate of the Sisters of St. Dominic took place in 1892. Stones for the foundation were shipped to the foot of the property. Since there were no paved roads, the stones were carried in relays to the site by the postulants and lay sisters. The cornerstone was laid in May of 1893.

Additional property was purchased in 1909 for building expansion. Thirty-one additional acres were purchased from nearby landowners. Mercedes Hall, pictured here on the upper right, was constructed in 1915. The three-story building contained a theatre, auditorium, and a dormitory for boarders of Mount St. Dominic Academy, as well as tennis courts. The building was demolished in 1929 and replaced by Aquinas Hall.

CALDWELL COLLEGE, CALDWELL, N. J.

The Sisters of St. Dominic had long desired to establish a college at Mount St. Dominic. Finally, in 1939, with the permission of Archbishop Thomas J. Walsh and the filing of a certificate of incorporation with the secretary of the State of New Jersey, Caldwell College for Women became a reality. The first class of 40 young women came together on September 19, 1939, and met a faculty of 12.

Three

BUILDINGS

The 1927 location of the A&P was at the corner of Gould Place and Bloomfield Avenue. Standing on the corner are Alfred Petrulio and his daughter Rosalind. Mr. Petrulio, a real estate developer, built and owned the building. He was brought to the U.S. from Italy as a small child by an uncle who was associated with the Monomonock Inn.

This view is of the McChesney residence and bakery with Roseland Avenue in the background. Part of the house was used as a bakery until about 1910. The borough took possession of the house in the mid-1920s and used it for municipal offices and a police station. After being torn down in the early 1937s, it is now a parking lot for Caldwell firemen.

The borough offices were located in "McChesney Hall" until, with the exception of the police department, they were transferred to this new municipal hall in 1938. In the fall of 1939, the police department moved to the municipal hall after the old building was razed.

44

Beginning in 1804, there were many attempts to establish a library. In 1894, the high school housed a library for public use. Finally, in 1907, the borough council, with the approval of the voters, requested a free public library. The building was ultimately constructed with a grant from the Carnegie Foundation and dedicated on October 12, 1917.

The first post office in the area was established in The Brick Store, West Caldwell, in 1819, with John L. Hudson as postmaster. For many years it moved about as politics and economics dictated. Ultimately, a permanent post office building was opened on Park Avenue in Caldwell on October 19, 1935, with William Quinn as postmaster.

A permanent home was established for the West Caldwell Library by a gift in the will of Mrs. Julia H. Potwin, nee Crane. Mrs. Potwin not only provided for the establishment of a library, she also left land for the library site and an adjoining plot, the present Crane Park.

This historic howitzer cannon stood in front of the Julia Potwin Library in West Caldwell from 1927 until 1941, when it was donated to the scrap drive for the war effort. Inspecting the cannon's arrival were Horace Welshman, Weldon Barton, Mayor Charles Nutting, Borough Clerk William Jacobus, and Police Chief William King.

The Caldwell Borough Improvement Association was organized in 1901 with the intention of cleaning up the undesirable conditions in the township. Association Hall was built in 1902 on a plot of land owned by the Caldwell Athletic Club adjoining the Methodist church. In 1922, the Caldwell Borough Improvement Association became the Women's Club of Caldwell, the same year the Association Hall burned to the ground.

After the fire, the Women's Club found temporary rooms in the Provost Homestead, now Provost Square, where they met for several years.

In 1928, the Women's Club built a new clubhouse, designed by architect C. Willard Wands, at the corner of Westville and Brookside Avenues, where it remains today. The Caldwell Women's Club Building is the oldest continuously occupied women's club in the state.

In October 1897, after a fire destroyed the wooden buildings opposite Roseland Avenue, Charles Canfield built the first brick building in Caldwell. The building, located at 295 Bloomfield Avenue, became known as the Hasler Building.

Prior to World War I, the post office was located in the Hart Building on the corner of Brookside and Bloomfield Avenues, c. 1913. B.A. Mathews operated the two stores on the right for the sale of groceries and footwear, while the post office was located on the left side.

A horse and carriage waits in front of a tobacco store on the corner of Hanford Place and Bloomfield Avenue. The Smith Building, as it was known then, was the second brick building in Caldwell and appears much the same today. Neighborhood houses of Hanford Place, some now gone, can be seen behind the building.

In the late 1700s, patrons came from Warren, Morris, and Sussex Counties to trade grain and flour for groceries at The Brick Store in West Caldwell. In 1819, the building served as the Caldwell Post Office. After many transfers of ownership, the building was purchased by the West Caldwell Council in 1915 and modernized for the headquarters of the Borough of West Caldwell and housing for the firetruck. The Brick Store was demolished in 1968. A signpost erected in 1980 designating the store site still stands at the corner of Cohen's Stationery parking lot.

The Brick Store became the borough hall and continued as such until 1936, when the building at the corner of Fairfield Avenue and Clinton Road was leased and then purchased for a new borough hall as expansion continued.

Four

COMMERCE

Caldwell's first bank was organized in 1903 and located on Bloomfield Avenue opposite Roseland Avenue. Hoffman's Pharmacy shared the ground floor at 289 Bloomfield Avenue and for many years the telephone company operated its Caldwell exchange on the second floor. The bank later moved its operation to the corner of Bloomfield Avenue and Personette Street.

In 1924, with the expansion of the banking business, the Caldwell National Bank was prompted to build larger quarters on the corner of Personette Street and Bloomfield Avenue. The sign in the window, to the left of the Corinthian columns, reads "West Essex Building & Loan," which had offices in the bank. Ekeman's Stationery can be seen behind the vintage car, and above Ekeman's is the law office of George Vanderdecker. Trolley tracks, cobblestones, and neat white crossing lines contributed to the clean appearance of the avenue, c. 1930. (Photo courtesy of Sam Kent.)

The Citizens National Bank, located at 391 Bloomfield Avenue in the Smith Building near Hanford Place, moved to this new building at the corner of Bloomfield and Smull Avenues. The building was dedicated January 16, 1915.

In 1926, the bank found the premises to be too small and work began to construct an addition on the east side. The Masonic Hall is visible at the rear right side of the building.

The T.F. Harrison Retail Hardware Store was located at 275 Bloomfield Avenue. The door on the left leads to the upstairs offices of Morris Lindsley, a well-known civil engineer at the time. The three bearded gentlemen on the front steps are neatly dressed in the business fashion of the time. The site is now occupied by the Meyer Building near Forest Avenue.

In 1907, the shoemaker shop at 439 Bloomfield Avenue was operated by Michael Livolsi, pictured at right. On the left is Henry Messina, a future Caldwell barber, and his brother Michael; both became longtime residents of the Caldwell area.

Around 1890, Fred and Frank Baldwin operated a meat delivery service in North Caldwell. They bought the meat in Paterson and Newark and kept it fresh in an icehouse on their property. The horse knew the route so well that he automatically stopped at each customer's house. The Baldwins were among the earliest settlers in this area.

Fritz's was a refreshment stand located at the trolley loop, the end of the line, at Bloomfield and Central Avenues. The stand, which faced Central Avenue, catered to neighborhood residents, as well as the many tourists who looked to the trolley as a ride out into the country. In this c. 1910 photo, Bert Belder, whose parents operated the store, is taking a break from his duties.

Arlington Russell operated this store in the early 1920s. The store, located opposite Roseland Avenue, was famous for the aroma of roasting peanuts, which was directed to the street through the hole visible below the front window. Mr. Russell's principal business was blacksmithing from his shop on Westville Avenue.

John T. Hull, proprietor of the John T. Hull Store, stands in front of his grocery store located at 379 Bloomfield Avenue, between Park Avenue and Hanford Place. The store was sold to the National Grocery Company and then managed for many years by Albert Holmquist. Mr. Hull's son Jack, recently deceased, was well known around town for 80 years. The photo was taken *c.* 1912.

The blacksmith shop of Harry Kanouse was located at 658 Bloomfield Avenue, near the West Caldwell center. This *c.* 1915 photo shows apprentice Joe Smith, Robert Lockward, and Mr. Kanouse. In his honor, the side street next to the building was named Kanouse Place.

Horace Welshman's store was opened in 1888 and located on the northeast corner of Bloomfield and Fairfield Avenues, West Caldwell. The store sold farm tools, groceries, dry goods, food, and grain. During the 50 years it was in business, the store was patronized by local citizens and borough officials. Chief William King, Borough Clerk William Jacobus, Mayor Herbert Francisco, and Sergeant Harry Price appear in this *c.* 1935 photo. The building survives today.

In 1911, *The Caldwell Progress*, the area's continuing weekly newspaper, occupied the right half of the Fischer Building at 380 Bloomfield Avenue opposite Hanford Place. The paper would make three moves before arriving at its present Brookside Avenue address.

West Essex Building & Loan Association was incorporated in 1915 when the first meeting of 84 stockholders was held. Arthur Jones was elected executive vice president and secretary. The first office and meeting place was located in the Caldwell National Bank from 1915 until 1935. From 1935 until 1948, the bank was located at 435 Bloomfield Avenue, as shown in the above photo. In 1948, the bank changed its name to West Essex Savings & Loan and moved to the opposite corner of Bloomfield Avenue and Cleveland Street, its present location and the former site of Gosman's Store. In the early years, it was common to obtain a mortgage from Mr. Jones after a 10-minute interview and a handshake. The bank is now called West Essex Bank.

Silent films were shown at 315 Bloomfield Avenue, which became a mecca for local residents wishing to see good entertainment. The house on the right in this c. 1914 photograph was that of Dr. Edward E. Peck. It was later moved around the corner to Personette Street and subsequently demolished for a bank parking lot.

CALDWELL THEATRE
CALDWELL, N. J.

The Home of the World's Best Photoplays
Accompanied by Music Befitting the Picture

E. H. METZGER, Mgr.

Show Days: Tuesday, Thursday, Friday and Saturday. Matinee at 3:15. Evening: 7:15 and 9:00 P. M.

Admission: Tuesdays and Fridays, Matinee—Children 6c, Adults 11c. Evening: Children 11c, Adults 17c. Thursdays and Saturdays, Matinee—Children 11c, Adults 17c. Evenings—Children 16c, Adults 28c.

Special Orchestra Every Thursday and Saturday
Patrons desiring our weekly program mailed to them, should leave their name and address at the box office.

PROGRAM

Tuesday, Dec. 2—Paramount presents

ENID BENNETT

in C. Gardner Sullivan's story

"STEPPING OUT"

Miss Bennett is seen in the role of a wife who invites the girl who was trying to win her husband, right into her own home in order to show the girl just what the husband really expected of a wife—to iron, scrub, cook, mend and economize. It was a daring experiment, but it worked out well. **Pathe News**

Harry Pollard in a funny comedy "Start Something"

Caldwell Theatre   Program Continued

Thursday, Dec. 4—Friday, Dec. 5—
Special Attraction—Two Days
William Fox presents the Greatest Racing Story Ever Filmed

"CHECKERS" (8 reels)

with an All-Star Cast, including

THOMAS CARRIGAN and JEAN ACKER

A special production of thoroughbreds and high life, intermingled with a basic drama of the human emotions. Adapted from the world famous novel of the same name, "Checkers" is the greatest story of the race-track and "sport of kings" ever filmed. It was more than three months in the making, the racing scenes having been taken at the famous Belmont Race Track, and an entire Jersey railroad rented for the big "wreck scene."

Extra on Thursday: Pathe News
A 2 reel Big V Comedy "Whiz and Whiskers"
Extra on Friday: Ford Weekly
Paramount-Braggs Comedy "Suprise Party and Everything"

Saturday, Dec. 6—William Fox presents
WILLIAM FARNUM
in a drama of love and adventure (6 parts)
"WOLVES OF THE NIGHT"
"Wolves of the Night" entered his life, stole his mine, and then in order to win the love of his wife, sent to Chile.   Bray Pictograph
Anne Luther in the 10th episode of "The Great Gamble"

This 1919 program presents the coming attractions of silent movies "accompanied by music befitting the picture."

In the early 1920s, the talkies came to a renovated Caldwell Theatre and filmgoers could see such stars as Jackie Coogan and Rudolph Valentino. John Musa operated the confectionery store to the left and Aaron Weckstein owned a shoe store on the right.

CALDWELL THEATRE

Vol. IV.   WEEK OF DECEMBER 1, 1919   No. 52

DOLORES CASSINELLI

This movie program was distributed weekly to the patrons.

The old movie house was displaced in May of 1925 by the Park Theatre at the corner of Forest and Bloomfield Avenues, shown here around 1950, looking westward.

On the hot, sultry Sunday of July 14, 1974, despite the heroic efforts of several volunteer fire departments of the area, the landmark Park Theatre was destroyed by fire, leaving the area without a movie theatre. (Photo courtesy of Gene Collerd.)

This photograph, taken about 1918 in front of 19 Orton Road (then known as Harrison Street), West Caldwell, shows the delivery truck of for the R.L. Crane Hardware Store in Caldwell. Mrs. Raymond L. Crane, whose husband owned the hardware store, is pictured holding her daughter Ruth, who became Mrs. Ralph H. Shepard.

Crane & Hicks opened a hardware store in 1910. R.L. Crane bought it in 1916 and eventually sold it to Warren Norris and William Schanz in 1924. Mr. Norris's son Robert joined his father at the store in 1948 after he graduated from Dartmouth. To accommodate the business growth, they moved the store in 1956 across the street to larger quarters, where H.E. Schanz Company Hardware remains a local tradition. After the death of his father in 1958, Robert took over the business.

Grunings, the popular ice-cream parlor, was originally located on Bloomfield Avenue before moving further west closer to Brookside Avenue. The store was famous for its Easter and Valentine candy and fine chocolates, as well as that delicious vanilla ice cream. The new location became a favorite meeting place and often the first place of employment for many of the young people.

This c. 1925 photo shows Ralph Leonard at the counter and George Thorward ready to serve the clients at the Park Sweet Shop. The shop was located in the Park Theatre building at the corner of Forest and Bloomfield Avenues. Years later, Mr. Thorward owned Thorwards Diner, a family eatery located at 253 Bloomfield Avenue, opposite Provost Square.

Thorward's Diner was a popular place at dinner time. Families would gather to dine and visit with friends, old and new. A comfortable, clean, and friendly place, Thorward's Diner was sadly missed when its doors were closed. The steeple of the Baptist church can be seen in the background.

This local A&P, with Depression-era prices, was managed by Thomas Quinn (left) and Howard Beam (the clerk), shown here ready to serve their customers. The aroma of freshly ground A&P Eight O'Clock coffee was sure to be in evidence.

In 1928, Mountain Motors, a Pontiac dealer, was located at 41 Bloomfield Avenue to the east of the town on "the flats." The salesmen in this photo are displaying the new models and are eager to sell. Van Note's Garage occupied the right part of the building.

Flowers, palms, and oriental rugs greeted the customers for the 1931 Chevrolet models at the showroom of Siggins Chevrolet, located on Bloomfield Avenue across from St. Aloysius Convent, which later became Fittin-Tully.

Frederic R. Cook housed both his furniture store and funeral parlor, a common combination, in this building on the corner of Personette Street and Bloomfield Avenue. The building was willed by Mr.Cook to the American Legion. The Cook funeral business later became the Dancy Funeral Home and eventually moved to Smull Avenue, where it is still located. Also visible in the above picture is Straub & Youngman Plumbing, which operated in town.

The Caldwell Barber Shop, located at 281 Bloomfield Avenue, was owned by Charles Sutera. Shown here c. 1929 are his assistants, Gus Prestifilippo and Jack Lombardi, who later owned their own shop.

John W. Gosman operated this spacious hardware store at 417 Bloomfield Avenue, at the corner of Cleveland Street, advertising general merchandise and farm implements. Notice the construction; it was not unusual in that era for a store to be higher than the sidewalk by four or five steps. One of the oldest stores in town, Gosman's was run for a time by Ernest Hines and then returned to the Gosman family. John's daughter, Ruth Gosman, also conducted the business. The building was demolished in 1947 to make way for West Essex Savings & Loan.

Five

STREETS AND
RESIDENCES

Located on Grandview Place in North Caldwell, the estate of Ernestine Schumann-Heink was purchased in 1905 from William Ryle, a Paterson silk manufacturer. The world-famous contralto was a kind and generous neighbor, hosting the September 10, 1912 concert at the Presbyterian church in Caldwell for the benefit of the Grover Cleveland Memorial Fund. This sold-out performance, with approximately nine hundred people attending, raised a considerable amount of money for the purchase of the birthplace. Some years later, Mme. Schumann-Heink gave a second recital for maintenance of the historic site.

This dwelling once stood at the corner of Bloomfield and Fairfield Avenues in West Caldwell and was occupied by the family of William Welshman, a Civil War veteran who died in 1913. Later, Horace Welshman took it over and operated a grocery store and barber shop in the basement.

Mr. Arlington Russell's family occupied this house at the corner of Westville Avenue and Runnymede Road in about 1900. Later, when George Canfield owned the property, the dwelling was torn down and a white stucco residence was constructed.

Lewis Grover Lockward and his wife, Anna Maria Crane, pictured here on the porch, owned this elegant house on Bloomfield Avenue. The house was constructed in 1874 and remodeled about 1900. St. Aloysius parish purchased this house and an adjoining one to build a convent. Lewis Lockward was Caldwell's first mayor (1892–94). His grandson, Donald G. Lockward, was mayor from 1951 to 1960.

Next door, to the left of the Lockward mansion, stood the home of Edmund P. Backus, which later became the home and office of Dr. E.C. Butler on Bloomfield Avenue.

This is the home of Noah and Naomi Baldwin as it appeared before the Civil War. It is located at the north end of Forest Avenue, on Mountain Avenue, formerly known as "Aunt Naomi's Lane."

Much of the early structure still remains, although years of renovation have altered its appearance to a large extent. The Baldwin home was built in 1793 by the great-great-greatgrandfather of the late Dean A. Baldwin and his brother, Personette G. Baldwin of North Caldwell.

This long-forgotten landmark on the southern side of Bloomfield Avenue, near Brookside Avenue, Caldwell, was known as the Gould House. Pictured above is its owner, Amos C. Gould, with his daughters: Charlotte Canfield, Jennifer Backus, and Elizabeth Harrison. Another daughter, Harriet Budd, was the mother of Ivon Budd of Caldwell. The homestead was built in 1805 and dismantled in about 1924. The Gould farm ran west from a site near Brookside Avenue to past Academy Road. Gould Place, Elizabeth Street, and Thomas Street are named for the family.

This 1908 postcard shows the corner of Westville Avenue and Washburn Place. The sign advertises plots and houses for sale or rent in "Caldwell Cedars." The area was developed by the American Homes Company under the management of Harry Steinhoff.

"The Caldwell Cedars" derived its name from the beautiful cedar trees that were so plentiful in the area. Taking advantage of the natural beauty of the tract, the roadways were laid out in gentle curves; houses were architecturally consistent with the environment and set so far apart that each had an air of privacy and its share of the beautiful cedar trees. Each house offered all modern conveniences and an "outdoor" sleeping porch on the second floor.

Both of these roads were laid out before the Revolution. Roseland Avenue going south was once called Centerville Road, and Westville Avenue going southwest was called the "Road from Samuel Crane's to the Meeting House." Westville Avenue was an important road in the developing of West Caldwell. Pictured on the left is the McChesney House; the man on the right is walking past the Slayback-VanOrder business office.

In 1910, Hatfield Street was just a meandering country road. On the left, the beginning of Grover Lane is visible. Grover Lane led to "Crow's Nest," the Corbiere's estate. Mrs. James K. Corbiere, the wife of the president of the trolley company, was the daughter of Thomas L. Smull. Most of the houses shown are still standing. The street was named after prominent landholder Caleb Hetfield. The spelling was altered in a clerical mishap.

This is an early postcard view of Hanford Place, *c.* 1908, as an old dirt road running toward Whitfield Street in Caldwell. Most of the buildings are still standing, although one has been removed for a parking lot. The home and office of Dr. and Mrs. Paul Reilly is visible at the end of the street on Whitfield Street.

In 1907, Forest Avenue was a dirt road and traffic was at a minimum. The sidewalks and telephone poles were already in place at the time. This street was originally known as Baptist Church Street for the church on the corner of Bloomfield Avenue. The road led to lots owned by the Presbyterian Church, where firewood was cut for the parsonage and the church.

As with most of the streets in the borough, *c.* 1910, Washburn Place had well-built and well-maintained houses. Dirt roads, sidewalks, and hitching posts are visible in this photo.

This is the typical tax bill a resident of the borough of Caldwell would receive in the year 1911.

This quaint unpaved road with beautiful homes is Wakefield Place looking from Park Avenue toward the present Central Avenue.

This view shows the corner of Gould Place and Westville Avenue, c. 1910, when the area was beginning to be developed. The tree-lined street and uncurbed dirt road present a rustic scene in the Caldwell Cedars.

After a public hearing in 1911, Farrington Street, Hillcrest Road, and Ravine Avenue were accepted as borough streets. Known as the Westover Tract, they represented a major development in the borough of Caldwell.

This view of the Westover Tract is looking east on Ravine Avenue.

Looking north toward Bloomfield Avenue on Brookside Avenue c. 1910, one would notice the open brook running alongside the street. Foot bridges or heavier structures built to carry a horse and carriage across the walled brook are visible as well. Looking much like today's parking meters, hitching posts are visible along the street. The brook is one of two originating in North Caldwell. They join on Westville Avenue in front of the current Women's Club building, and flow into the Grover Cleveland Park Pond to become Pine Brook before moving on to the Passaic River.

SOME OF CALDWELL'S PROGRESSIVE BUSINESS HOUSES

Architect.
Lynn G. Lockward............237 Bloomfield Ave.

Automobile Garages.
Bush's Garage.................43 Roseland Ave.
Caldwell Garage, Klein & Brown 271 Bloomfield Ave.

Bakers.
Richard A. Carr..............370 Bloomfield Ave.
Fentzlaff's Caldwell Bakery....360 Bloomfield Ave.

Banks.
Caldwell National Bank.......289 Bloomfield Ave.
Citizens National Bank........391 Bloomfield Ave.

Bicycles, Repairs, Sporting Goods.
A. P. Clark..................409 Bloomfield Ave.

Boarding Houses.
The Trewmont, F. A. Tipping, Prop...Central Ave.
Rates $2 Per Day.
The Hillside House, Mrs. Mary Jacobus.Hillside Ave.

Cigars, Toys, Stationery, Ice Cream, Etc.
Moran & Kane...............283 Bloomfield Ave.

Carpenters and Builders.
Wilbur B. Gould.................26 Cleveland St.
J. E. Hamilton...................39 Roseland Ave.
Samuel D. Harrison..............18 Cleveland St.
Samuel Hawk.....................Brookside Ave.
E. T. Rathbun....................Caldwell, N. J.
G. H. Stryker....................Caldwell, N. J.

Civil Engineers and Surveyors.
Charles H. Matthews...............65 Elm Road
J. S. Provost.................235 Bloomfield Ave.

Coal, Wood and Ice.
Slayback-Van Order Co..........7 Oak Grove Road
Stephen J. Speer..............105 Roseland Ave.

Dairies.
Henry Becker.....................Roseland, N. J.
J. M. Harrison..............West Caldwell, N. J.

Druggists.
William N. Hasler............295 Bloomfield Ave.
Carl E. Hoffman.............287 Bloomfield Ave.

Local businesses and their street addresses were listed under "*Some of Caldwell's Progressive Business Houses.*" This listing was taken from a booklet published by the Caldwell Board of Trade in 1913.

In this *c.* 1925 postcard, the business section between Forest Avenue and Personette Street shows still another location for the Atlantic & Pacific Company Grocery Store in addition to Lasser's Drug Store. The number of cars parked at the curb depicts an active shopping area.

On the left of this photo is the corner of Brookside and Bloomfield Avenues, its buildings looking much as they do today. The wide, bending road offers much room for the horses, trolley cars, and automobiles—and there were no meters!

This *c.* 1916 view of a rather neat Bloomfield Avenue shows a quiet, picturesque town. Curbing and fire hydrants are visible, with a good width for all modes of transportation. The corner of Brookside Avenue, on the left, looks very much as it does today.

The American Food Company was located on Bloomfield Avenue opposite Park Avenue. It was the epitome of the old-fashioned grocery store. Tabs were run for customers, clerks gathered the items one by one on a shopper's list, and such specials as "ground bones, five cents" were offered.

This turn-of-the-century photo, taken looking east on Bloomfield Avenue with the trolley tracks in the foreground, shows another location of the post office, which adjoined the wheelright shop where I. Halsey Budd was manager. The American Food Company is the adjacent building, and the house in the background with the two chimneys is the Gould House.

I. H. Budd

BUSINESS WAGONS AND TRUCKS

MADE TO ORDER

BLOOMFIELD AVENUE
ADJOINING POST OFFICE

Caldwell, N. J

The business card of the wheelright, I. Halsey Budd, describes the address—not with street numbers—but according to the nearest landmark.

BLOOMFIELD AVE. WEST OF WASHBURN PL., CALDWELL, N.J.

This is a view of Bloomfield Avenue near the corner of Cleveland Street The hardware store of John W. Gosman is on the left side of this picture. That building was torn down to make way for the West Essex Savings & Loan building and an adjacent parking lot. The large white house on the right was moved around the corner to Gould Place, where it still stands today.

Academy St. & Bloomfield Ave., Caldwell, N. J.

This postcard shows a primitive view of a horse and buggy in front of the Methodist church heading toward Academy Road, while the trolley tracks follow Bloomfield Avenue leading to the terminal. The triangle creating the fork in the road, wooded at the time as Monomonock Inn property, is now the site of a service station.

Bloomfield Avenue opposite Roseland Avenue is pictured here in 1918. The unpaved road had Belgian blocks for the trolley tracks. A horse-drawn water wagon kept the dust down in the summer. Visible in this photo are Lasser's Drug Store, Kane & Moran Confectionery Store (note the sign for Castle's Ice Cream), and the Caldwell National Bank.

This early 1900 photo postcard renders a peaceful view of an uncluttered Bloomfield Avenue with only one pedestrian and a horse and carriage in sight. The Caldwell Presbyterian Church is visible on the left, the borough's first brick building is on the right, and graceful elm trees line the street.

The horse-drawn wagon as well as the horseless carriage, *c.* 1908, have no traffic or parking problems on Bloomfield Avenue. This view is looking west from Forest Avenue opposite Roseland Avenue.

This historic view of Bloomfield Avenue at Hanford Place was taken looking east from Gould Place, *c.* 1907. The Smith Building, visible on the left, was the second brick building built in Caldwell and is still in existence, as is the one on the opposite corner.

This is Bloomfield Avenue, c. 1885. The beautiful photo presents a newly built stone Presbyterian church, a dusty dirt road, and men and boys assembled in front of the post office and telegraph office at the Caldwell Pharmacy.

An 1890 map of Caldwell named the landowners and their boundaries. Note that Park Avenue was named Central Avenue.

Six

BOARDING HOMES AND HOTELS

Built in 1782 for the minister of the Presbyterian congregation, the lower part of the building was used as a parsonage by the Reverend Stephen Grover from 1787 until 1800. After a succession of owners, it was sold to Sarah E. Beach in 1864, who enlarged the home and ran it as a boarding house. The hotel was located between Forest and Arlington Avenues and was eventually acquired by the Sisters of St. Dominic in 1888 to serve as a temporary school, infirmary, and convent. The building was torn down in 1913.

Grover House, Caldwell, N. J.

The Grover House was built by the Reverend Stephen Grover as the church-manse in 1817. It was located between Personette Street and Smull Avenue. In later years, the house was transformed into a hotel and boarding house and was a popular vacation place for many years. The annex at the rear left became the Masonic Hall on Smull Avenue. The Grover House was razed in the early 20th century to clear the site for the Citizens National Bank.

The Caldwell House was located on Bloomfield Avenue opposite Brookside Avenue. It was built as a tavern by Aaron Crane in 1803 to provide rest and refreshment for the charcoal and tan-bark wagoners on their way to and from Newark and the northern counties. It was bought, renovated, and enlarged by the addition of two upper stories by A.A. Snyder in 1882. Later it was purchased by John A. Brady and run as a hotel until 1928, when the upper part was destroyed by fire and the street floor converted into stores. For many years, this building housed the only saloon in town and was known as the Brady House.

The Hillside House, *c.* 1912, was located on Hillside Avenue between Hatfield and Crane Streets. It accommodated 35 guests at rates of $2 to $3 per day and was just one of the many hotels and inns operating in Caldwell as summer resorts in the early 1900s.

Caldwell, New Jersey

One of the Three Healthiest Spots in America

Published by the
CALDWELL BOARD OF TRADE
1913

Printed by The Caldwell Progress, Caldwell, N. J.

A promotional booklet published in 1913 by the Caldwell Board of Trade names the area as "One of the Three Healthiest Spots in America."

Mr. J.W. Phyfe built this summer house, located elegantly on the bluff of Academy Road, in the spring of 1893 at a cost of approximately $18,000. Mr. Phyfe was a vigorous opponent to the trolley. When approval was given to build the trolley line, he lost his interest in Caldwell.

The Wilson Hotel was located on Roseland Avenue at the Essex Fells line. The hotel later became known as the Oaks and Idelwild. With the passing of time, it was torn down and replaced by an apartment complex at 178 Roseland Avenue.

For many years, the borough of Caldwell was a favorite place for summer guests. There were private homes, small hotels, and a showcase hotel, the Monomonock Inn, built and operated by the Outlook Hotel Company. The inn opened its doors for guests on June 7, 1902.

The Monomonock Inn, the essence of grandeur, is pictured here. It featured 55 sleeping rooms, a billiard room, a library, a parlor, and a dining room, all tastefully furnished.

The Monomonock Inn, which crowned the bluff on Prospect Street and Academy Road, featured a magnificent view up and down the valley for miles.

The gardens at the old Monomonock Inn, which took up an entire block bounded by Bloomfield Avenue, Prospect Street, and Academy Road, were an outstanding feature of this popular summer resort. This view taken from the east portion of the grounds shows the sunken formal gardens.

These photos depict the serenity of a summer day at the inn.

The inn had a nine-hole golf course on the west side of Prospect Street, a putting green, and tennis courts. Note here that both men and women, graciously attired, used the putting green. The long-time golf pro in attendance was Tom Washington.

Monomonock Inn   Caldwell, N. J.

The kitchen for the inn was detached from the main building. The south end of the building was originally the Phyfe residence, visible here on the right. The large inn was dismantled in 1942 and 1943 except for the administration building. The MaryAnn Apartments were constructed on the site in 1945.

Looking majestic at the top of a small hill is another of Caldwell's boarding homes. The elegant Knoll Rest, with mansard roof and balconies, was located on Elm Road off Bloomfield Avenue. The house was formerly owned by Robert C. Ryerson, one of the first councilmen of the Borough of Caldwell and a trustee of the Caldwell Presbyterian Church. The structure was razed in the early 1950s to allow the construction of the present brick apartment complex.

Seven

INDUSTRY AND
TRANSPORTATION

Crane's Saw Mill, one of the original mills predating the Revolutionary War, was operated by the Cyrus Crane family for more than 160 years. The mills of the area enabled the transformation of trees into building timber, allowing frame buildings to be erected in old Caldwell.

Crane's Saw Mill, located on Passaic Avenue, was owned by the Crane family and passed on for five generations. A water wheel provided power until the mill converted to diesel power in the late 1940s. In 1967, Crane's Mill was dismantled and taken to Allaire State Park. The Crane homestead, however, remained on the original site.

Shown here is a painting of the William Crane Homestead by noted Caldwell artist Nat Lewis. The painting was the first of numerous prize-winning works by Ms. Lewis.

After erecting a cottage near his sawmill, Cyrus Crane raised a family of six children, four boys and two girls, all of whom worked the mill. This old industrial landmark is now only a memory.

Posing at Crane's Saw Mill in West Caldwell in this 1920 photo are Clifford Harrison, Marcus Crane (owner of the mill at the time), an unidentified workman, Ernest Haversang, and Clarence Harrison, the twin brother of Clifford. Part of their daily routine would be preparing enormous logs like this one for the mill.

The Lane & Lockward Tobacco Company, the most prosperous of the many tobacco companies in the area, operated from this building on Bloomfield Avenue in West Caldwell. The site was just west of the present Seven-Eleven store near the Sunnyside Apartments. This 1922 photo shows the rear of the factory, which faced Bloomfield Avenue. The small building at the rear is the powerhouse. The wagon was used to transport tobacco from Newark to the factory, where it was made into cigars and chewing tobacco.

The staff of the Lockward family's tobacco factory line up for the photographer in this 1911 photo. The youngster on the pony is Lewis G. Lockward; to the left is Robert C. Lockward. The principal business of the enterprise was the making of chewing and smoking tobacco with the production of cigars as a side line. The tobacco factory operated by Lane & Lockward was on the south side of Bloomfield Avenue. The building, torn down in 1931 to allow the widening of Bloomfield Avenue, was replaced by Sunnyfield Pool.

A trio of young media men discuss the news of the day. *The Caldwell Progress* publisher, W. Hilton (Hilt) Higgins, and editor, John A. (Jack) Sullivan Jr., conferred with Malcolm Forbes. *The Caldwell Progress* (now called *The Progress*) was first published in 1911 with William VanWart as publisher and editor.

The old mill wheel belonging to the Sindle Grist and Sawmill on West Greenbrook Road, North Caldwell, gave many years of service. It was one of five mills operating on Green Brook Road dating back to the 1800s. The millstone from the grist and sawmill was recovered in 1997 and will be used as a focal point at the community center on Gould Avenue. The approximate size of the mill can be determined by comparing it to the size of the man in the picture.

This beautiful aerial view shows the DeCamp Dairy Farm as it appeared in 1924. The two long barns on the hillside housed 150 dairy cows, while horses and hay were kept in the large barn in the right foreground. The farm was located on Runnymede Road near Westville Avenue, West Caldwell.

Originally Fairfield Dairy Farm, the DeCamp Dairy covered land from Runnymede Road to Orton Road and from Westville Avenue to Deerfield Road. The dairy was owned by George M. Canfield and later by Witsel DeCamp. Several men are shown here cutting green feed for cows around 1939 at the dairy.

The Slayback-Van Order Company, c. 1900, was a major supplier of coal, wood, lumber, and ice. The building, located on Bloomfield Avenue behind the Caldwell Railroad Station, was demolished in 1952.

Another major supplier of coal, wood, and ice was the S.J. Speer Company. At one time, Speer was located on Roseland Avenue where the railroad tracks crossed the road. In years to come, the company became a supplier of home heating oil. The Speer Fuel Company was destroyed by fire in 1969.

This extraordinary photo taken on "Parsonage Bend," the eastern end of Bloomfield Avenue in Caldwell, presents three methods of transportation. The era of the steam engine was about to expire, and the last run for the trolley was to be March 30, 1952, when 50 new buses were put into immediate service. The tracks were not removed but covered with asphalt to better accommodate the most recent mode of transportation shown here—the automobile. (Photo courtesy of Railroad Avenue Enterprises.)

In this *c.* 1902 photo, Charles Conklin stands beside a hack that ran from Caldwell to Pine Brook and other ports of call. Mr. Conklin operated his horse and buggy until the autobus and automobile taxi came into common use.

An ice-wagon waits across the tracks at the Slayback-VanOrder lumber yard in the area of Bloomfield Avenue and Elm Road. In 1912, steam locomotives, visible to the right, were housed here in sheds.

Even with the arrival of the trolleys, the horse and carriage prevailed for many years. Mr. Jacobus provided a delivery service with destinations from Newark to Caldwell. Shown here are various types of wagons used (depending on the need), his staff, and his horses. This service was located on Campbell Avenue, which is Central Avenue today.

CALDWELL & MONTCLAIR STAGE LINE.

TIME TABLE TO TAKE EFFECT

Monday, October 2, 1871.

		A.M.	P.M.
Leave	CALDWELL,	7.20	2.30
"	VERONA,	7.35	2.45
"	MOUNT PROSPECT,	7.55	3.05
Due at	MONTCLAIR,	8.10	3.20
"	NEWARK,	8.35	3.50
"	NEW YORK,	9.15	4.25
		A.M.	P.M.
Leave	NEW YORK,	8.40	3.50
"	NEWARK,	9.20	4.30
Due at	MONTCLAIR,	9.45	4.51
"	MOUNT PROSPECT,	10.10	5.20
"	VERONA,	10.25	5.35
"	CALDWELL,	10.40	5.50

NOTE—Carriages can be had at Caldwell, by applying to the driver, or at the Stable.

GEO. B. HARRISON, Prop.

CALDWELL Sept. 18th, 1871.

The Caldwell and Montclair Stage Line was started by P.H. Harrison, who sold to George B. Harrison and was succeeded by James Husk in 1883. It took only two hours to travel from Caldwell to New York by stage in 1871, a good time considering the travel was by a horse-drawn stagecoach. This line continued up until the time the trolley car came into existence. At that point, Mr. Husk gradually retired from the business.

This 1914 International Harvester Bus owned by Marcus DeCamp and operated, as shown here, by Harold "Duke" DeCamp, made runs from Roseland Center to Hoffman's Drug Store at the Caldwell National Bank. The operation was suspended during World War I.

This Jitney bus traveled between Caldwell and Roseland and at times to Livingston. Pictured at the wheel on a summer day in 1910 is Percy Williams, the owner of the Jitney bus.

This *c.* 1904 picture shows one of the first DeCamp buses, which originally ran only between Caldwell and Roseland, but later extended to Livingston. Mary Jacobus, who ran a confectionery store in Caldwell, stands by.

Hoffman's Drayage Carting Company was based at 20 Washburn Place, appearing here in the background. Note that Charles Hoffman wore a jacket and tie when delivering for stores in the Caldwell area, *c.* 1930.

The automobile age arrived and with it came the first traffic light, a blinker light shown here on the corner of Roseland Avenue and Bloomfield Avenue. The flagpole and the cannon monument on the green were erected by the Borough with the consent of the Presbyterian Church Trustees in 1911 in memory of the soldiers from Caldwell who were killed in the Civil War. The library is visible in the distance, on the left.

After four years of strong opposition and legal maneuvers, the trolley line was finally opened and running on August 31, 1896. The first car was piloted by Mrs. James Corbiere (see p. 75). Note the cow catcher in front of this early trolley.

The trolley ran from this terminal to the Montclair-Verona line for a fare of 5¢. The trolley line was run by the North Jersey Street Railway Company, the predecessor to Public Service. In the summer during the early years of the trolley, open-sided cars were used.

TROLLEY STATION, CALDWELL, N.J.   M12733

This trolley is ready for the return trip to the top of the first mountain. Montclair refused to grant permission for the laying of the rails within its borders, so a stage took passengers to the trolley line in Glen Ridge to travel to Newark.

114

When Montclair finally completed its trolley line in 1899, it enabled the riders to go directly to Newark from Caldwell without changing cars. In 1927, the line would acquire the route number 29. As the Caldwells grew, so did the trolley line operation. More frequent running times and larger cars were provided. This became the preferred method of commuter travel.

This "work" trolley left the terminal at Central Avenue to repair and maintain the tracks as well as trolley cables. Its purpose was the general maintenance necessary to keep the trolley lines in operation.

This picturesque view looking down from Arlington Avenue displays a charming railroad station. The motherhouse of the Sisters of St. Dominic is visible up the hill; the dominant windmill and a horse and carriage from Fears Freight and Baggage Express complete the picture.

Railroad Station, Caldwell, N. J.

This wooden railroad station was strategically constructed opposite Arlington Avenue on the bend of "the Big Road." The freight trains visible at the rear would be bringing supplies to the area.

Erie R. R. Cut, Caldwell, N. J.

This steam locomotive is headed west from the Caldwell Station to the turntable in Essex Fells that positioned the locomotive to face east for the return trip. Behind the new cut in the hill, the active windmill is visible.

CALDWELL

Erie Station, Caldwell, N. J.

Passengers waited for the train at the station on the edge of a tree-lined Bloomfield Avenue. In this bucolic small-town view, a horse and buggy are visible on the right side of the avenue in front of the Grover Cleveland Birthplace.

Erie Station, Caldwell, N. J.

This all-encompassing view taken from "Parsonage Hill" gives a fine panoramic picture of a busy Erie Station. The path to Mount St. Dominic is also visible behind the windmill. After 74 years of operation, the Erie-Lackawanna Railroad discontinued passenger service from Caldwell on October 3, 1966.

Eight

AROUND THE TOWNS

This mural appears on the wall in the council chambers of the Caldwell Administration Building. The mural was painted by the art students of James Caldwell High School.

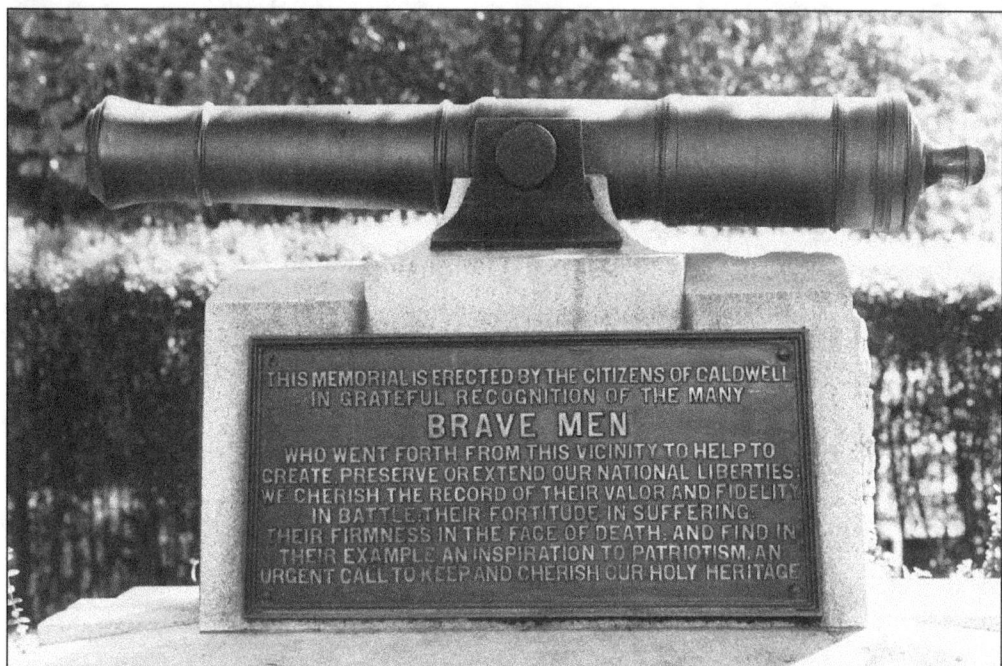

The cannon on the green is a replica of the original cannon presented to Caldwell by Colonel Peter Decatur in 1824. The original mounted cannon was stolen in 1968.

This is a traditional Memorial Day parade on Bloomfield Avenue. Spectators line the street as the marching band proudly passes by. (From the collection of William Dietrich.)

Prospect Hill Cemetery is located on Westville Avenue and Thomas Street. Many of the historic names mentioned in this book can be found on the tombstones standing in this cemetery. The first interment was in 1866 and the grounds are still being used today.

Young men and women are assembled for a 1932 picture while participating in the West Caldwell Students Week. This was an annual observance during which the young people assumed municipal posts.

This 1914 photo shows the Passaic Valley Squad Farm, which later became the Puritas Water Company. In 1929, the Trecartin family founded a swim club and named it for the large elm tree (which is now long gone), along with the impressive Puritas water tower.

Many generations of families enjoyed the sun and fun at this longtime favorite facility on Central Avenue in West Caldwell.

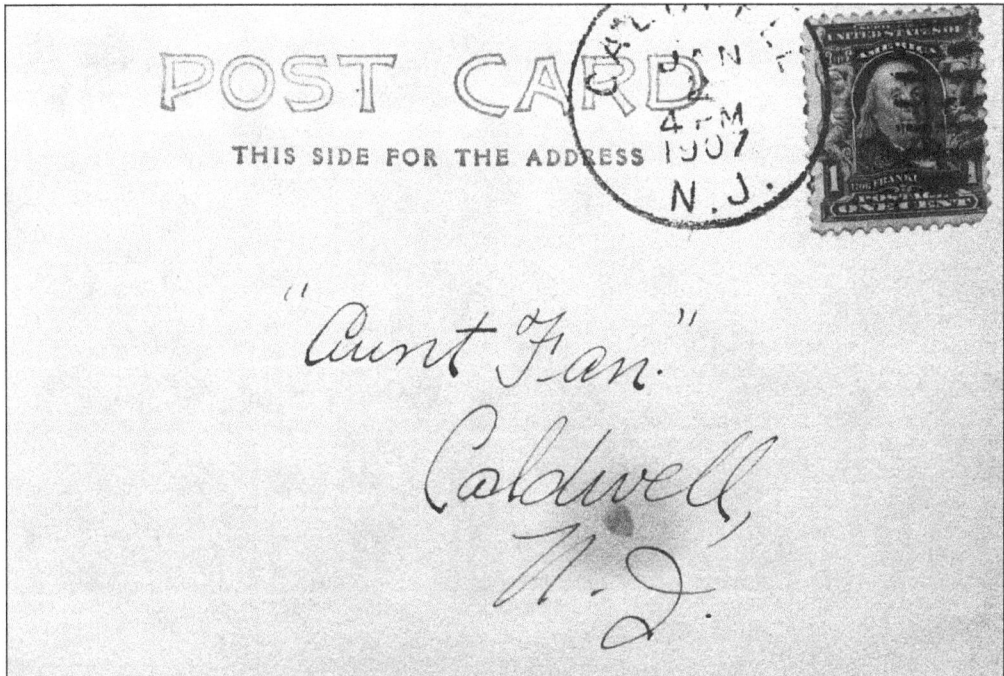

THIS SIDE FOR THE ADDRESS

"Aunt Fan."
Caldwell,
N. J.

"Aunt Fan" received her postcard in 1907. The card was delivered with the very simple address seen here—her first name, town, state.

A winning baseball team! The Caldwell Athletic Club posed in September of 1935 after winning the Essex County League Championship two out of three years. Team members are, from left to right, as follows: (kneeling) Bob Sweeney, Harry Jacques, Jerry Romano, Johnny McEntgee, Eddie Sempf, Jack Tighe, and ? MacDonald; (standing) Nick Mullick, manager Peter Scorso, Charles Nevin, Bob Ivanicki, Packy McDaniels, Stan Stankavich, Ace Miller, Vic Lynch, and Jack Hugh.

In 1965, under Mayor Newton Winans, the name of Progress Square was changed to Provost Square. "Ted" Provost, pictured here in the wheelchair, witnessed the ceremony. The Kiwanis Oval and the surrounding property were at one time the Provost estate and homestead.

Posing here is the Caldwell High School Class of 1924.

THE RHINELAND GARDENS
641 Bloomfield Ave., West Caldwell, N. J.
Kurt Schmitz, Prop.   Tel. Caldwell 6-0717
Dine and Dance :: German Atmosphere
An ideal spot for picnics and outings

The Rhineland Gardens, located opposite Lane Avenue, was a noted restaurant and catering establishment in its day. Later it became "The Well"; it is now the site of the Atrium apartment complex.

This spontaneous celebration took place on Bloomfield Avenue. The happy faces around Caldwell on August 14, 1945, were due to the announcement of victory over the Japanese. The celebrants are on the avenue opposite the Presbyterian church in front of Lasser's Pharmacy.

For many years, the traditional Kiwanis Kapers annual fund-raiser was the highlight of the fall season. Preparing for the 1951 presentation are, from left to right, Wally Colross, Mayor George Kaplan, Mayor Bill Dodge (kneeling), Robert Larsen Jr. and Sr., and photographer James Young. Kiwanis received its charter in 1924 and its first president was Dr. J.C. Conover.

Celebrating the completion of the foundation of the Knights of Columbus Hall on Personette Street, c. 1930, are Mr. Gagliano, Joseph Prestifilippo, Santo Stivali, and Joseph LoPresto. In the spirit of brotherhood, members of the Knights of Columbus held their meetings at the Masonic Hall for six and one half years prior to the construction of their own building.

126

A neighborly looking group gathers at the Cloverleaf Tavern, c. 1942. Proprietor George Dorchak tends to his customers. Located on Bloomfield Avenue near Hanford Place, the Cloverleaf remains a family-type restaurant where locals and out-of-towners come to enjoy the camaraderie.

BACH FAMILY HOME

The original stone portion of the house was erected in 1774 and was purchased by Charles Bach in 1865. The property remained in the Bach family for 100 years. Ralph Bach was one of the founders of North Caldwell in 1898. Civic participation has since remained a Bach family tradition.

NORTH CALDWELL BICENTENNIAL COMMISSION

The section of the area commonly called Bushtown remained part of Caldwell Township until March 31, 1898, when it was incorporated as the Borough of North Caldwell. Dr. Oliver P. Dawson was chosen as the first mayor. This signpost is visible designating the historic home of the Bach family, located at 498 Mountain Avenue, North Caldwell.

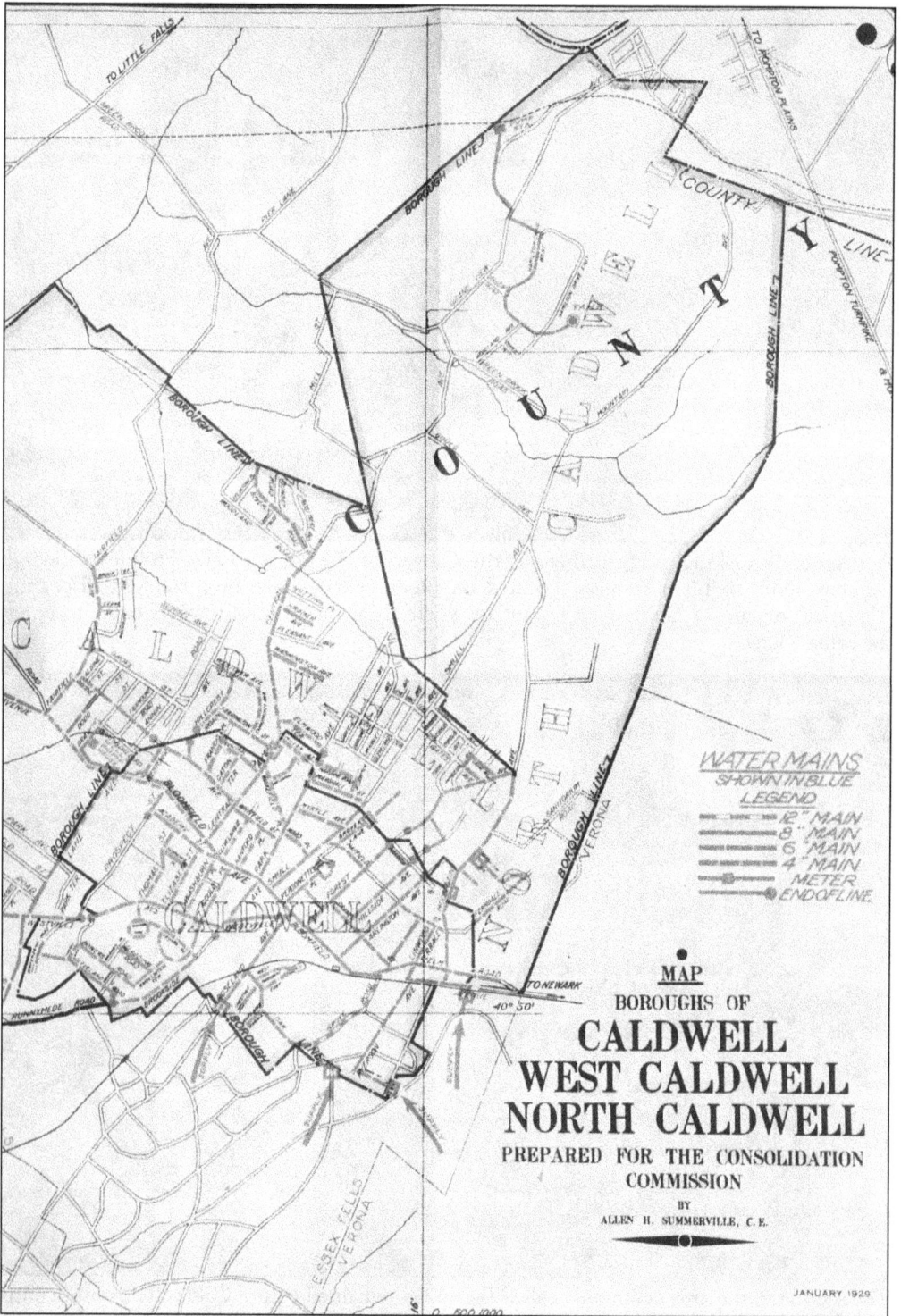

This 1929 map prepared by Allen Summerville was drawn up for the consolidation of the Caldwells.